...CAL • GUITAR

WORLD'S G[illegible]ST
ROCK HITS

35 Favorites from Rock's Biggest Superstars

From classic rock to red-hot modern hits, this collection of more than 200 pages of sheet music guarantees a lifetime of musical enjoyment for music makers of all ages. Universal crowd pleasers range from perennial favorites by Led Zeppelin, Nirvana, Pink Floyd, and The Rolling Stones to contemporary hits from a huge array of modern superstars, including Green Day, Muse, Radiohead, and more.

Alfred

Produced by
Alfred Music Publishing Co., Inc.
P.O. Box 10003
Van Nuys, CA 91410-0003
alfred.com

Printed in USA.

ISBN-10: 0-7390-6988-8
ISBN-13: 978-0-7390-6988-2

Cover Photos
Synthesizer and drums: © istockphoto.com / Don Bayley • Guitar: © istockphoto.com / Simon Podgorsek • Crowd: © Redferns • Rock Concert: © istockphoto.com / Josh Perkins

Alfred Cares. Contents printed on 100% recycled paper.

CONTENTS

21 GUNS

Lyrics by
BILLIE JOE

Music by
GREEN DAY

B♭
C
yourself suf - fo - cat - ing?
breaks the spir - it of your soul.
Verses 2 & 4:
Dm
B♭
F
C
2. Does the pain weigh out the pride?
4. Your faith walks on bro - ken glass,
Dm
B♭
F
C
Dm
B♭
And you look for a place to hide?
and the hang - o - ver does - n't pass.
Did some-one break your
Noth-ing's ev - er
F
C
B♭
C
heart in - side? You're in ru - ins.
built to last, you're in ru - ins.

Chorus:
F C/E Dm C B♭ F
One, twen - ty - one guns, lay down your arms, give up the fight.
(Ah.
C F C/E Dm C
One, twen - ty - one guns, throw up your arms
)
B♭ F C
in - to the sky, you and I.
(Ah.)
B♭ F 1. C 2. C
(Ah.))

Bridge:
Dm Bb F C Dm Bb
Did you try to live on your own, when you burned down the
F A Dm Bb F A
house and home? Did you stand too close to the fi - re? Like a li -
Bb Csus C
ar look - ing for for - give - ness from a stone.
Guitar solo:
F C/E Dm C Bb F

C
F
C/E
Dm
C
B♭
F
C
B♭
F
A
Dm
B♭
F
C
Dm
B♭
F
C
subito mp
Verse 5:
Dm
B♭
F
C
Dm
B♭
5. When it's time to live and let die, and you can't get an -
mf

F C Dm B♭
oth - er try.
Some - thing in - side this
F C B♭
heart has died, you're in ru - ins.
Chorus:
F C/E Dm C B♭ F
One, twen - ty - one guns, lay down your arms, give up the fight.
(Ah.
C F C/E Dm C
One, twen - ty - one guns, throw up your arms
)

B♭ F C F C/E
into the sky. One, twenty-one guns,
(Ah.)
Dm C B♭ F C
lay down your arms, give up the fight.
(Ah.)
F C/E Dm C B♭ F
One, twenty-one guns, throw up your arms into the sky,
(Ah.
C B♭ F C
you and I.
)
(Ah.)

BEAT IT

Written and Composed by
MICHAEL JACKSON

*Original recording sounds a half step lower than written.

D C D
dis - ap-pear." The fire's__ in their eyes and their words are real - ly clear. So
be a man. You wan - na stay a - live; bet - ter do what you__ can. So
Em D Em
beat it, just beat it. You bet - ter run, you bet - ter
beat it, just beat it. You have to show them that you're
D Em D
do what you can. Don't wan - na see no blood. Don't be a ma - cho man. You
real - ly not scared. You're play - in' with your life. This ain't no truth or dare. They'll
C D Em
wan - na be tough, bet - ter do what you can. So beat it. But you
kick you, then they beat you, then they'll tell you it's fair. So beat it. But you

Chorus:
D Em D
wan - na be bad.
wan - na be bad.
…end solo)
Just beat it, (beat it,) beat it, (beat it.) No
Em D Em
one wants to be de - feat - ed. Show - in' how funk - y and strong
To Coda
D Em D
is your fight. It does - n't mat - ter who's wrong or right. Just
1.
Em D Em D
beat it, just beat it, just beat it, just beat it.

2.
Em
D
Em
D
beat it, (beat it,) beat it, (beat it.) No___ one wants to be de - feat - ed. Show-
Em
D
Em
D
in' how funk - y and strong__ is your fight. It___ does-n't mat-ter who's__ wrong or right. Just
E5
D
beat it, beat it, beat it, beat it,
E5
D
beat it, beat it, beat it,

E5
D
beat it, beat it.
E5
D.S. 𝄋 al Coda
𝄌 Coda
Em
D
Em
D
beat it, (beat it,) beat it, (beat it.) No___ one wants to be de-feat - ed. Show-
Repeat ad lib. and fade
Em
D
Em
D
in' how funk-y and strong___ is your fight. It___ does-n't mat-ter who's___ wrong or right. Just

25 OR 6 TO 4

Words and Music by
ROBERT LAMM

Moderately bright rock ♩ = 144

Verse:
Am Am/G Am/F♯ F E
1. Wait-ing for the break of day,
2. Star-ing blind - ly in - to space,
3. Feel-ing like I ought to sleep,
Am Am/G Am/F♯ F E
search-ing for some things to say.
get - ting up to splash my face.
spin-ning room is sink - ing deep.
Am Am/G Am/F♯ F E
Flash-ing lights a - gainst the sky,
Want-ing just to stay a - wake,
Wait-ing for the break of day,
Am Am/G Am/F♯ F E
giv - ing up, I close my eyes.
won-d'ring how much I can take.
search-ing for some - thing to say.

Chorus:
F
C
Sit-ting cross - legged on the floor,
Should I try to do some more,
Twen-ty - five or six to four;
To Coda
1.
G
F
twen-ty - five or six to four.
Am
Am/G
Am/F♯
F
E
Am
Am/G
Am/F♯
F
E

2.
F
Am
Am/G
Am/F♯
Solo ad lib.
Repeat as desired
Last time
D.C. al Coda
Coda
F
E
F
E
F
Am
Am/G
Am/F♯
F
E
Solo ad lib.
D2
Cm(9)
B6
G7/B♭
B/A
molto rit.

BITTERSWEET SYMPHONY

Lyrics by
RICHARD ASHCROFT

Written by
MICK JAGGER and KEITH RICHARDS

E
Bm7
Asus
A
sim.
mf
1.
2.
Verse:
1. 'Cause it's a (3.) bit - ter - sweet
er prayed, but to - night
sym - pho - ny, this life.
I'm on my knees, yeah.
Try'n' to make
I need to
ends meet, you're a slave to mon - ey, then you die.
hear some sounds that rec - og - nize the pain in me, yeah.
(3.) try to find some - bod - y, then you die.

Asus A E Bm7 Asus A
I'll take you down the on - ly road I've ev - er been
I let the mel - o - dy shine, let it cleanse my mind. I feel free,
E Bm7 Asus A E Bm7
down. You know, the one that takes you to the
now. But the air - waves are clean and there's no -
Asus A E Bm7 Asus A
plac - es where all the veins meet, yeah.
bod - y sing - ing to me, now.
Chorus:
E Bm7 Asus A
No change, I can't change, I can't change, I can't change, but I'm here

E Bm7 Asus A
in my mold, I am here in my mold. But I'm a
E Bm7 Asus A
mil - lion dif - f'rent peo - ple from one day to the next, I can't change
To Coda
1.
E Bm7 Asus A E Bm7
my mold, no, no, no, no, no, no.
Have you ev - er been down?
Asus A E Bm7 Asus A
2. Well, I've nev -

2.
Asus
A
E
Bm7
no, no, no. I can't change, no, no, no,
Have you ever been down?
Asus
A
E
Bm7
Asus
A
D.S. 𝄋 al Coda
I can't change it.
3. 'Cause it's a
Coda
Asus
A
E
Bm7
no, no, I can't change my mold, no, no, no,
Asus
A
E
Bm7
no, no. I can't change my mold, no, no, no,

Asus
A
E
Bm7
__ no, no.___ It's just - a sex and vio - lence, mel -
I can't change… (etc.)
Asus
A
E
Bm7
Asus
A
o - dy and si - lence. Just - a sex and vio - lence, mel - o - dy and si - lence. Just - a… (etc.)
I'll take you
E
Bm7
Asus
A
down___ the on - ly road___ I ev - er been___
E
Bm7
Asus
A
Repeat ad lib. and fade
___ down. I'll take you

BLITZKRIEG BOP

Words and Music by
JEFFREY HYMAN, JOHN CUMMINGS,
DOUGLAS COLVIN and THOMAS ERDELYI

A
Ay! Oh! Let's go! Ay! Oh! Let's go! They're
Verse:
A D E A
form - ing in a straight line. They're go - ing through a tight wind.
D E A D5 E
The kids are los - ing their minds. The Blitz - krieg
A D A
Bop! They're pil - ing in the back - seats.

D
E
A
D
E
To Coda
They're gen - er - at - ing steam heat.
Pul -
A
D
E
A
D
A
sat - ing to the back - beat.
The Blitz - krieg Bop!
Chorus:
D
A
Ay, oh, let's go, shoot 'em in the back, now.
D
A
D
What they want, I don't know._ They're

B
1.
D
E
2.
D
E
D.S. 𝄋 al Coda
all revved - up and ready - y to go.
They're
read - y to go.
They're
𝄌 Coda
A
D5
E
A
D
A
sat-ing to the back - beat.
The Blitz - krieg Bop!
N.C.
Ay! Oh! Let's go! Ay! Oh! Let's go!
(Drums only)
A
Ay! Oh! Let's go! Ay! Oh! Let's go!

BORN TO RUN

Words and Music by
BRUCE SPRINGSTEEN

Bsus
E
At night we ride through mansions of glory in
Just wrap your legs 'round these velvet rims and
A
Bsus
A
suicide machines. Sprung from cages on
strap your hands 'cross my engines. Together we could
E/G♯
F♯m
E/G♯
Highway Nine, chrome-wheeled, fuel-injected, and steppin' out over the line.
break this trap. We'll run till we drop, and, baby, we'll never go back.
E
D/E
A
Oh, baby, this town rips the
Oh, will you walk with me out on the

E/G♯
F♯m
E/G♯
bones from your back. It's a death trap, it's a su - i - cide rap.__ We got - ta
wire? 'Cause, ba - by, I'm just a scared and lone - ly rid - er, but I
E
C♯m
A
get out while__ we're young.__ 'Cause tramps__ like us,
got to know__ how it feels. I want to know if love is wild, babe, I
B
E
ba - by, we were born__ to run.
want to know if love__ is real.
f
A
Bsus
B
E

A
1.
Bsus
B
2.
Bsus
B
2. Wen - dy,
E
A
B
Sax. solo:
E
A
B
C♯m
B
E
Bm7
Be -
mf

Bridge:
Dsus D Dsus D Gsus G
yond the Pal - ace, hem - i - pow-ered drones scream down the bou - le - vard.
Gsus G Asus A Asus A
Girls comb their hair in rear - view mir - rors and the
Csus C Csus C Dsus D
boys try to look so hard. The a - muse-ment park ris - es
Dsus D Gsus G Gsus G
bold and stark as kids are hud-dled on the beach in the mist. I wan - na

Asus A Asus A Csus C Csus C
die with you, Wen-dy, on the streets to-night in an ev-er-last-ing kiss.
Huh!
Fsus F Fsus F Fsus F Csus C
f
Fsus F Fsus F F♯sus F♯
F♯sus F♯
N.C.

One, two three, four! 3. The
Verse 3:
E
A
high-way's jammed_ with bro - ken he-ros on a last - chance pow-er drive.
Bsus
B
E
Ev - 'ry - bod - y's out on the run___ to-night, but there's
A
Bsus
B
A
no place left to hide.___ To - geth - er, Wen - dy, we can

E/G♯ F♯m E/G♯
live with the sad - ness, I'll love you with all___ the mad - ness in my
E D/E A
soul.___ Oh,___ some-day, girl,___ I don't_
E/G♯ F♯m E/G♯
___ know when, we're gon - na get to that place where we real - ly wan - na
E C♯m A
go, and we'll walk in the sun. But till then, tramps like us,

B
E
C♯m
4
ba - by, we were born to run.
Ah, hon - ey,
A
B
E
tramps like us,
ba - by, we were born to run.
C♯m
4
A
B
Come on, Wen - dy.
Tramps like us,
ba - by, we were born to
E
A
run.
Whoa.

Bsus B E A
Hmm, oh, oh, oh, oh.
Bsus B E A
Whoa, oh, oh, oh, oh. Hmm.
Bsus B E A
Whoa. Whoa.
B E
Whoa, oh, oh, oh, oh.
rit.

BRING ME TO LIFE

Words and Music by
BEN MOODY, AMY LEE
and DAVID HODGES

Em
ing some - where___ cold, un - til you find___ it there_ and lead_
___ me.________ Breathe___ in - to me_____ and make_ me real,_
Am/E
1.
To Next Strain
N.C.
______ it back home.
______ bring
2.
N.C.
To Next Strain
3.
me to___ life._________ me to
Chorus:
Em
G
(3rd time:) life. Wake_ me up___ in - side,________ wake_ me up___ in - side._
(Wake me up.) (I can't wake up.)

D
Em
Call my name and save me from the dark.
(Save me.)
G
Bid my blood to run before I come undone.
(Wake me up.)
(I can't wake up.)
D
1. Em
D.S. 𝄋
Save me from the nothing I've become.
(Save me.)
2.3. Em
C
D
nothing I've become. Bring me to

To Coda
Em
life.
(I've been liv - ing a lie.__)
(There's noth - ing in - side.)
C
D
Em
Bring me to life.
Bridge:
Am
Em/G
B7sus/F♯
Em
Fro - zen in - side__ with - out__ your touch,__ with - out__ your love,______ dar - ling. On -
Am
Em/G
B7sus
D.S. 𝄋 al Coda
ly you______ are__ the__ life____ a - mong_ the dead.______________

Verse 3:
All this time I can't believe I couldn't see.
Kept in the dark, but you were there in front of me.
I've been sleeping a thousand years, it seems.
Got to open my eyes to everything.
Without a thought, without a voice, without a soul.
Don't let me die here.
There must be something more.
Bring me to life.
(To Chorus:)

COMFORTABLY NUMB

Words and Music by
ROGER WATERS and DAVID GILMOUR

A
Come on, now,___ I hear you're feel - ing___ down.___ Well,
(Come on, come on.___)
2. O - kay, (O - kay, o - kay.___) just a lit - tle pin - prick. There'll be no more...
G
Em7
Bm
I can ease your pain,__ get you on your feet a - gain.__
("ah,"___) but you may feel a lit - tle sick.__ Can you
Bm
A
Re - lax, (Re - lax, re - lax.___) I need some in - for - ma - tion first.___
stand up? (Stand up, stand up.___) I do be - lieve it's work - ing. Good.__ That - 'll keep you

G
Em7
Bm
Just the ba - sic facts,_ can you show me where_ it hurts?
go - ing for_ the show._ Come on, it's time_ to go.
Chorus:
D
A
There is_ no pain,_ you are_ re - ced - ing._
mf
D
A
G/B
A dis - tant ship's_ smoke on_ the ho - ri - zon._
C
G
You are on - ly com - ing through_ in waves._ Your
sim.

C
G
lips move,_ but I can't hear_ what you're say - ing.
1. When
3. When
D
A
I was a child, I had_ a fe - ver. My
2. (Gtr. solo ad lib....
I was a child, I caught_ a fleet - ing glimpse,_
D
A
G/B
hands felt_ just like_ two_ bal - loons._
out_ of the cor - ner of my eye._
C
G
Now I've got_ that feel - ing once_ a - gain._ I_ can't ex - plain, you would not un -
I turned_ to look,_ but it_ was gone,_ I can - not put_ my fin - ger on_

C
G
der - stand, this is not how I am.
it now. The child is grown, the dream is gone.
...end solo)
A
G/B
C
G
I have be - come com - f'rta - bly
1.
2.
D.S. 𝄋
3.
D
D
D
numb.
numb.
numb.
cresc.
Repeat ad lib. and fade
Bm
A
G
Em
Bm
(Gtr. solo ad lib.)

CREEP

Words and Music by
THOMAS YORKE, JONATHAN GREENWOOD,
PHILIP SELWAY, COLIN GREENWOOD, EDWARD O'BRIEN,
ALBERT HAMMOND and MIKE HAZELWOOD

Moderately ♩ = 92

B
could-n't look you in the eye.
I want to have con - trol.
You're just like an an -
I want a per-fect bod-
C
Cm
3
gel,
y,
your skin makes me cry.
I want a per - fect soul.
G
You float like a feath - er
I want you to no - tice
in a beau-ti-ful world.
when I'm not a-round.
B
C
I wish I were spe - cial.
You're so f*** - **' spe - cial.

Cm
You're so f***-**' spe - cial.
I wish I were spe - cial.
But I'm a creep,
Chorus:
G
B
I'm a weird - o.
C
What the hell am I do - ing here?
1.
Cm
I don't be - long here.
I don't care if it hurts,

2.
Cm
here, oh, oh.
Bridge:
G
B
She's running out the door.
C
She's running, she
Cm
G
run, run, run, run.

B
C
Cm
Run.
3. What-ev-er makes you hap-
Verse 3:
G
B
py,
what-ev-er you want.
mp
C
You're so f***-**' spe-cial.
I wish I were spe-

Cm
cial.
But I'm a creep,
Chorus:
G
B
I'm a weird - o.
C
What the hell am I do-ing here?
I don't be - long
Cm
here.
G
I don't be - long here.
rit.

DON'T STOP BELIEVIN'

Words and Music by
JONATHAN CAIN, NEAL SCHON
and STEVE PERRY

A
E
B
lone - ly world.
South De - troit.
cheap per - fume.
wants a thrill,
sing the blues.
She took the mid-night train go - ing
He took the mid-night train go - in'
For a smile they can share the night, it goes
pay - in' an - y - thing to roll the dice just
Oh, the mov - ie nev - er ends, it goes
1. 4.
G♯m
A
2.
D.C.
an - y - where.
one more time.
an - y - where.
3. 5.
B/A
on and on and on and on.
Strang - ers
Street - light
cresc.
f

B/A A B/E E B/E E
wait - ing, up and down the bou - le - vard, their
peo - ple, liv - ing just to find e - mo - tion,
1.3.
B/A A B/A A B/E E
shad - ows search - ing in the night.
hid - ing
2.4.
B/E E B/A A B E B E A
To Coda
some - where in the night.
E B C♯m7 A
D.S. 𝄋 al Coda

Coda
E
B
C♯m
A
(Inst. solo ad lib.…
E
B
G♯m
A
E
B
C♯m7
A
Don't stop believ-in', hold on to the feel-in'.
Repeat ad lib. and fade
E
B
G♯m
A
Street-light peo-ple.

EARTH SONG

Written and Composed by
MICHAEL JACKSON

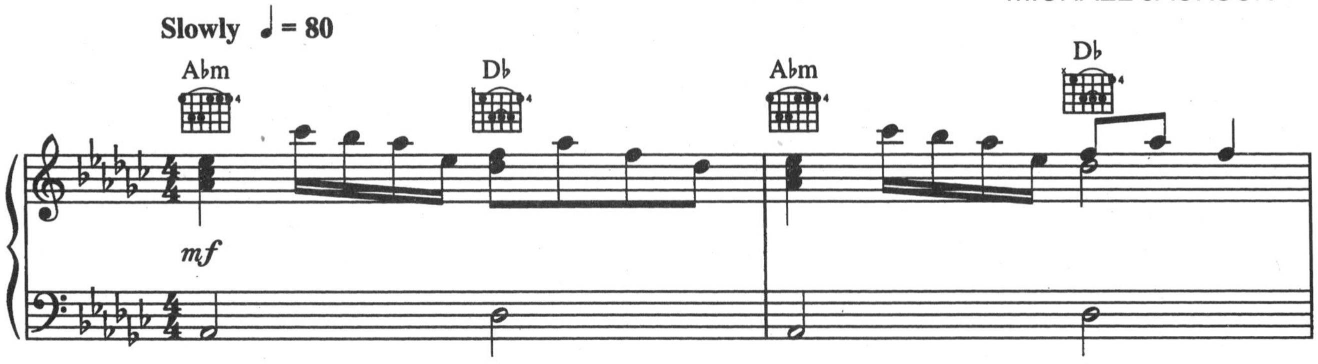

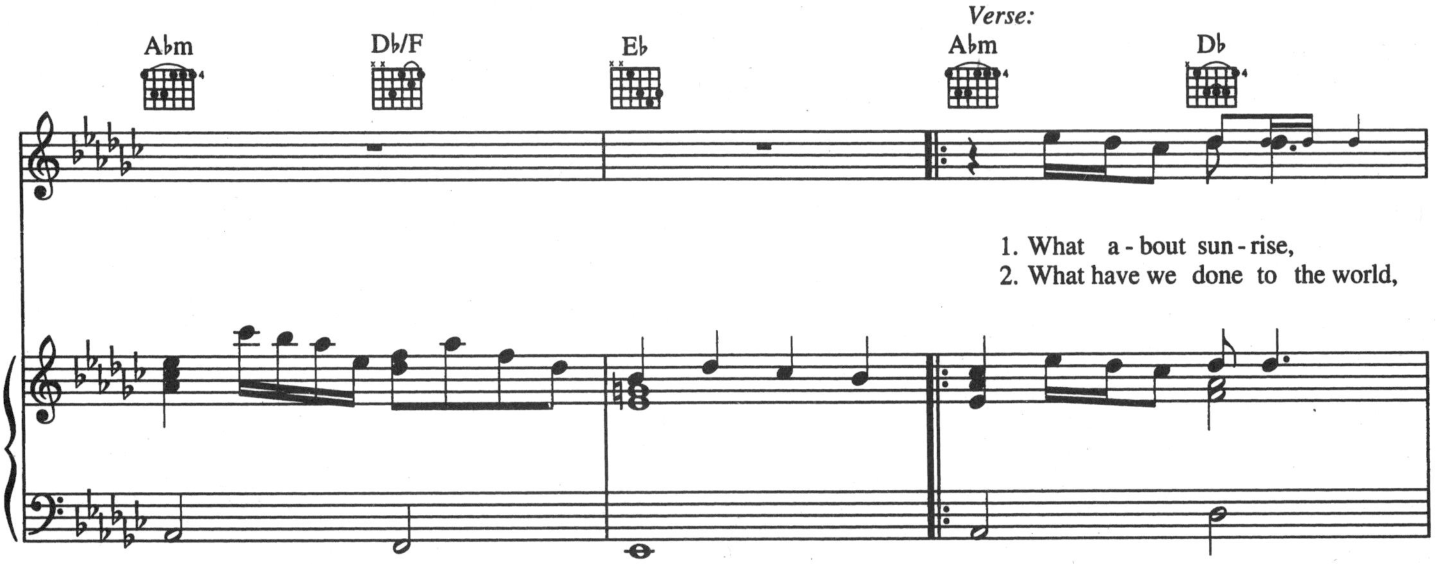

Eb
Abm
Db
Abm
Db
said we were_ to gain?_
pledge your on - ly son?_
What a-bout kill-ing fields,
What a-bout flow-ering fields,
is there a time,
is there a time?
Abm
Db
Eb
what a-bout all the things_ that you said was yours_ and mine?_
What a-bout all the dreams_ that you said was yours_ and mine?_
Did you
Did you
Dbm7
Gbsus
Gb
Cb
Abm
ev - er stop_ to no - tice all the blood we've shed_ be - fore?_
ev - er stop_ to no - tice all the chil - dren dead_ from war?_
Did you
Did you
Dbm
Eb
ev - er stop_ to no - tice the cry-ing Earth, the weep - ing shores?
ev - er stop_ to no - tice the cry-ing Earth, the weep - ing shores?
Ah,_

Chorus:
Abm
Db
Abm7
Db
Abm
Db
ah.
Ooh,
Abm7
Db
Abm
Db
Abm7
Db
ooh.
Ah,
ah.
Ooh.
Abm
Db
To Coda
1.
Eb
2.
Eb
Bridge:
Dbm7
Gbsus
Gb
Cb
Abm
I used to dream,
I used to glance be - yond the stars.

D.S. 𝄋 al Coda
D♭m
E♭
Now I don't know_ where we are,_ al - though I know we've drift - ed far._
Ah,_
Coda
E♭
B♭m
E♭
B♭m7
E♭
_ Ah,_ ah._ Ooh,_
B♭m
E♭
B♭m7
E♭
B♭m
E♭
_ ooh._ Ah,_
B♭m7
E♭
B♭m
E♭
F
ah._ Ooh._ 1. Hey,_

Bbm
Eb
Bm7
Eb
what a - bout yes - ter - day? (What a - bout us?) What a - bout the seas?_ (What a - bout
us?) 2.4. See additional lyrics
Bbm
Eb
Bm7
Eb
us?) The heav - ens are fall - ing down. (What a - bout us?) I can't e - ven breathe._ (What a - bout
Bbm
Eb
Bm7
Eb
us?) What a - bout the bleed-ing Earth? (What a - bout us?) Can't we feel its wounds?_ (What a - bout
Bbm
Eb
1.-4.
F
us?) What a - bout na - ture's worth? (Ooh, ooh.) It's our plan - et's womb. (What a - bout
3
3

Verse 2:
What about animals?
(What about it?)
We've turned kingdoms to dust?
(What about us?)*
What about elephants?
Have we lost their trust?
What about crying whales?
We're ravaging the seas.
What about forest trails,
(Ooh, ooh.)
Burnt despite our pleas?

Verse 3:
What about the holy land
(What about it?)
Torn apart by creed?
What about the common man,
Can't we set him free?
What about children dying?
Can't you hear them cry?
Where did we go wrong?
(Ooh, ooh.)
Someone tell me why.

Verse 4:
What about babies
(What about it?)
What about the days?
What about all their joy?
What about the man?
What about the crying man?
What about Abraham?
What about death again?
(Ooh, ooh.)
Do we give a damn?
(To Chorus:)

*Repeat after every line except where specified.

GOOD RIDDANCE
(Time of Your Life)

Lyrics by
BILLIE JOE

Music by
BILLIE JOE and GREEN DAY

Em
D
C (9)
G
So make the best of this test and don't ask why.
Tat - toos of mem - o - ries and dead skin on trial.
Em
D
C (9)
G
It's not a ques - tion, but a les - son learned in time.
For what it's worth, it was worth all the while.
...end solo)
It's
Chorus:
Em
G
Em
G
some - thing un - pre - dict - a - ble, but in the end it's right. I
Em
D
To Coda
G
hope you had the time of your life.

C2
D
G
C2
1.2.
D
3.
D
D.S. 𝄋 al Coda
It's
Coda
G5
C2
D5
G5
C2
D5
G5
rit.

GREAT BALLS OF FIRE

Words and Music by
OTIS BLACKWELL and JACK HAMMER

Rock and roll ♩ = 152

I laughed at love 'cause I thought it was fun - ny.
8va
Gliss.
F7
G7
You came a - long and you moved me, hon - ey.
I changed my mind,
F7
C
N.C.
this love is fine.
Good - ness gra - cious, great balls of fire!
F7
C
Kiss me, ba - by.
Hmm,
it feels

F7
good. Hold me, ba - by. Well,
8va
Gliss.
G7
I want to love you like a lov - er should. You're fine,
so kind. Got to tell this world that you're mine, mine, mine, mine.
C
F7
I chew my nails and I twid - dle my thumbs. I'm real nervous, but it
Gliss.

G7
F7
To Coda
sure is fun.
C-'mon, ba-by, you're driv-ing me cra-zy.
C7
N.C.
Piano solo:
C
Good-ness gra-cious, great balls of fire!
F7
8va
Glissando
Gliss.
G7
(8va)
Gliss.
F7
Gliss.
C

(8va)
F7
G7
(8va)
F7
C
D.S. al Coda
Well!
(8va)
Glissando
Coda
C7
N.C.
C
Good - ness gra - cious, great balls of fire!

HEY JOE

Words and Music by
BILLY ROBERTS

Moderately slow, with a half-time feel ♩ = 80

E
gun in your hand? Oh.
C
G
D
I'm go'n' down to shoot my old la - dy. You know I
A
E
caught her mess - in' 'round with an - oth - er man. Yeah.
C
G
I'm go - in' down to shoot my old la - dy.

D
A
E
You know I caught her mess - in' 'round with an - oth - er man.
Huh, and that ain't too cool.
Verse 2:
C
G
D
A
2. Hey, Joe,
I heard you shot your
3
E
To Coda
wom - an down, you shot her down now.

C
G
D
A
Hey, Joe, I heard you shot your
E
la - dy down, you shot her down to the ground.
C
G
D
Yeah. Yes, I did, I shot her. You
A
E
know I caught her mess - in' 'round, mess - in' 'round town.

C
Yes, I
G
D
A
did, I shot her. You know I caught my old la - dy mess - in'
E
'round town and I gave her the gun. I shot her!
C
G
D
A
E
All right!

C
G
Shoot her one more time a - gain for me.
D
A
E
Yeah!
Aw, hit it.
C
G
D
A
E
D.S. 𝄋 al Coda

Coda

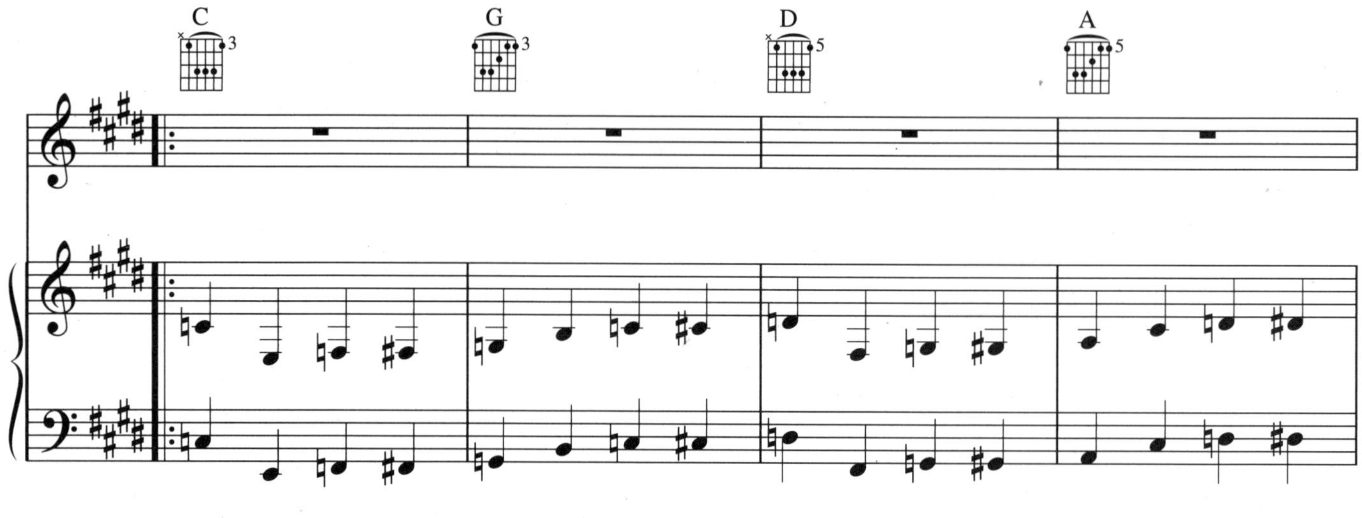

Verse 3:
Hey, Joe, said now,
Where you gonna run to now?
Where you gonna run to?
Hey, Joe, I said
Where you gonna run to now?
Where you gonna go?
Well, dig it!
I'm going way down south,
Way down to Mexico way!
All right!
I'm going way down south,
Way down where I can be free!
Ain't no one gonna find me, babe!
(To Coda)

HEY THERE DELILAH

Words and Music by
TOM HIGGENSON

G
A
Bm
Times Square can't shine as bright as you. I swear it's
We'll have the life we knew we would. My word is
A
A5
D5
true. Hey there, De - li - lah, don't you
good. Hey there, De - li - lah, I've got
F♯m
D5
wor - ry a - bout the dis - tance, I'm right there. If you get lone - ly, give this
so much left to say. If ev - 'ry sim - ple song I wrote to you would
F♯m
Bm
Bm/A
song an - oth - er lis - ten. Close your eyes.
take your breath a - way, I'd write it all.

G
A
Bm
A
A5
Lis-ten to my voice, it's my dis-guise. I'm by your side.
E-ven more in love with me, you'd fall. We'd have it all.
Chorus:
D5
D5/A
Bm
Bm/C♯
D5
D5/A
Oh, it's what you do to me, oh, it's what you do to me.
mf
Bm
Bm/C♯
D5
D5/A
Bm
Bm/C♯
Oh, it's what you do to me,
To Coda
1.
2.
D5
D5/A
Bm
Bm/C♯
D5
D5/A
Bm
Bm/A
oh, it's what you do to me. What you do to me. A

Bridge:
G
A
thou - sand miles seems pret - ty far, but they've got planes and trains and cars. I'd walk
D5
D5/A
Bm
Bm/A
to you if I had no oth - er way. Our
G
A
friends would all make fun of us, and we'll just laugh a - long be - cause we know
D5
D5/C♯
Bm
Bm/A
that none of them have felt this way. De -

G
A
li - lah, I can prom-ise you__ that by____ the time__ we__ get through,_ the world_
Bm
___ will nev - er, ev - er be the same,________________ and you're to blame._
A
Verse 3:
D5
F♯m
3. Hey there, De - li - lah, you be good__ and don't you miss__ me. Two more

D5
F♯m
Bm
Bm/A
years and you'll_ be done with school and I'll___ be mak-ing his-t'ry, like I do.
G
A
Bm
Bm/A
You know it's all be - cause of you.___
G
A
Bm
Bm/A
G
A
We can do what-ev - er we__ want___ to.______
Hey there, De-li - lah, here's to you._
Bm
A
A5
D.S. 𝄋 al Coda
___ This one's for you.

Coda
Bm
Bm/C♯
D5
D5/A
Bm
Bm/C♯
What you do to me.
Oh,
whoa,
D5
D5/A
Bm
Bm/C♯
D5
D5/A
Bm
Bm/C♯
whoa.
Oh,
whoa, whoa.
Oh,
D5
D5/A
Bm
Bm/C♯
D5
D5/A
D5
oh,
oh.

HOME SWEET HOME

Words and Music by
NIKKI SIXX, VINCE NEIL
and TOMMY LEE

C
Em
things went right, it does-n't mean they were al - ways wrong._ Just take this
C7/B♭
F/C
song and you'll nev - er feel___ left all a - lone._ Take me to your
C
Em
heart, feel me in your bones. Just one more
C7/B♭
F
night, and I'm com-ing off_ this long and wind - ing road._ I'm on my

Chorus:
A♭
B♭
C
way,_ I'm on my way,_ home sweet_ home. To -
A♭
B♭
night, to - night,_ I'm on my way,_ I'm on my way,_ home sweet_
f
Verse 2:
C
C
home. 2. You know_ that I've seen too man - y ro -
Em/B
C7/B♭
F/C
man - tic dreams_ up in lights, fall - ing off_ the_ sil - ver screen. My heart's_ like an

C
Em/B
C7/B♭
o - pen book for the whole_ world to read._ Some-times noth-ing keeps me to-geth-er
Chorus:
F/C
A♭
B♭
at the seams. I'm on my way,___ I'm on my way,___ home sweet_
C
A♭
home. To - night, to - night,_ I'm on my way,_ just set me
B♭
C
B♭
free,_ home sweet_ home. Home sweet_
(Inst. solo ad lib.…

A♭
B♭
C
B♭
home.
Home sweet_ home.
Home sweet_
A♭
1.
B♭
2.
B♭
home.
Oh,__ I'm on my
A♭
B♭
C
way, I'm on my way,_ home_ sweet_ home._______
A♭
Yeah,________ I'm on my way,___ I'm on my

B♭
C
way, home sweet home.
C
Em/B
C7/B♭
mf
F/C
C
Em/B
Hmm, hmm, hmm
C7/B♭
F/C
hmm hmm, oo - oo.
rit.

HOTEL CALIFORNIA

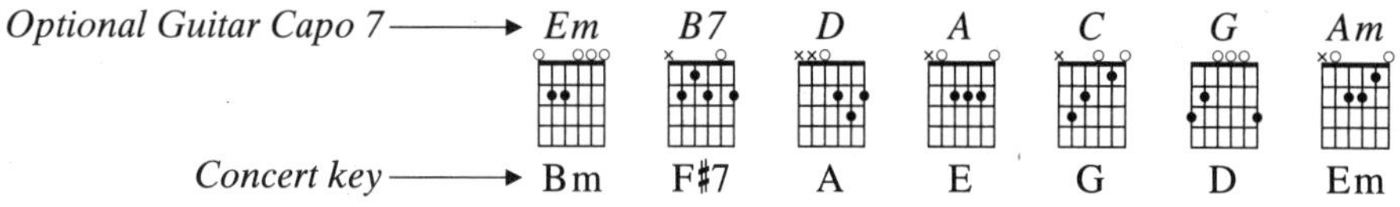

Words and Music by
DON HENLEY, GLENN FREY
and DON FELDER

1.
2.
Em
F#7
F#7
Verses 1 & 2:
Bm
F#7
1. On a dark des-ert high-way, cool wind in my hair,
2. Her mind is Tif - fa - ny twist - ed, she got the Mer - ce - des bends.
mf
A
E
warm_ smell of co-li - tas_ ris - ing up through the air._
She got a lot of pret-ty, pret-ty boys_ that she calls friends._
G
D
Up a - head in the dis - tance, I saw a shim-mer-ing light.
How they dance in the court - yard, sweet_ sum-mer sweat.

Em
F#7
My head grew heav - y and my sight grew dim,
Some dance to re-mem - ber,
I had to stop for the night.
some dance to for - get.
Bm
F#7
There she stood in the door - way,
So I called up the cap - tain,
I heard the mis - sion bell.
"Please bring me my wine."
He said,
A
E
And I was think - ing to my - self, "This could be
"We have - n't had that spir - it here since
heav - en or this could be hell."
nine - teen six - ty - nine.
G
D
Then she lit up a can - dle
And still those voic - es are call - ing from
and she showed me the way.
far a - way,

Em
F#7
There were voic - es down the cor - ri - dor,
wake you up in the mid - dle of the night
I thought I heard them say,
just to hear them say,
8
Chorus:
G
D
"Wel - come to the Ho - tel Cal - i - for - nia!
Such a
F#7
Bm
love - ly place, (such a love - ly place,) such a love - ly face.
They're
G
D
Plen - ty of room at the Ho - tel Cal - i - for - nia,
liv - in' it up at the Ho - tel Cal - i - for - nia.
an - y
What a

Em
1.
F♯7
time_ of year_ (an-y time_ of year_) you can find_ it here._
nice_ sur-prise,_ (what a nice_ sur-prise,_) bring your
2.
F♯7
N.C.
Verse 3:
Bm
al - i - bis._
Mir-rors_ on the ceil - ing,_
mp
F♯7
A
the pink cham-pagne on ice,_ and she said,
"We are all just pris-on-ers here_
3
E
G
of our own_ de-vice."
And in the mas - ter's_ cham - bers,_

D
Em
they gath-ered for the feast.
They stab it with their steel - y knives, but they
F♯7
Bm
just can't kill the beast.
Last thing I re-mem - ber, I was
F♯7
A
run-ning for the door.
I had to find the pas-sage back to the
E
G
place I was be - fore.
"Re-lax," said the night - man.
"We are

D
Em
— pro - grammed_ to re - ceive.
You can check out an - y - time you like,
F#7
N.C.
Solo:
Bm
3
but you can__ nev - er leave."__
(Inst. solo ad lib....
(Cue notes 2nd time only)
F#7
A
E
G
D
Em

1.2.
F♯7
3.
F♯7
…end solo)
Bm
F♯7
A
E
G
D
Em
F♯7
Repeat and fade

HOW SOON IS NOW?

Moderately ♩ = 92

Words and Music by
STEVEN MORRISSEY
and JOHNNY MARR

of nothing in particular.
...end solo)
Chorus:
G A A2 C
A B B2 D
1.2.6. You shut your mouth.
3.4.5. See additional lyrics
G A2 Bsus D2
A B2 C♯sus E2
How can you say I go about things the wrong
E A2 C
F♯ B2 D
way? I am human and I need to be loved

G
A2
Bsus
D2
To Coda
A
B2
C♯sus
E2
just like ev - 'ry - bod - y else does.
E
F♯
G
A
E
A
B
F♯
1.
2.3.
4.
D.S. al Coda
G
A
G
A
G
A
A
B
A
B
A
B
2. I am the

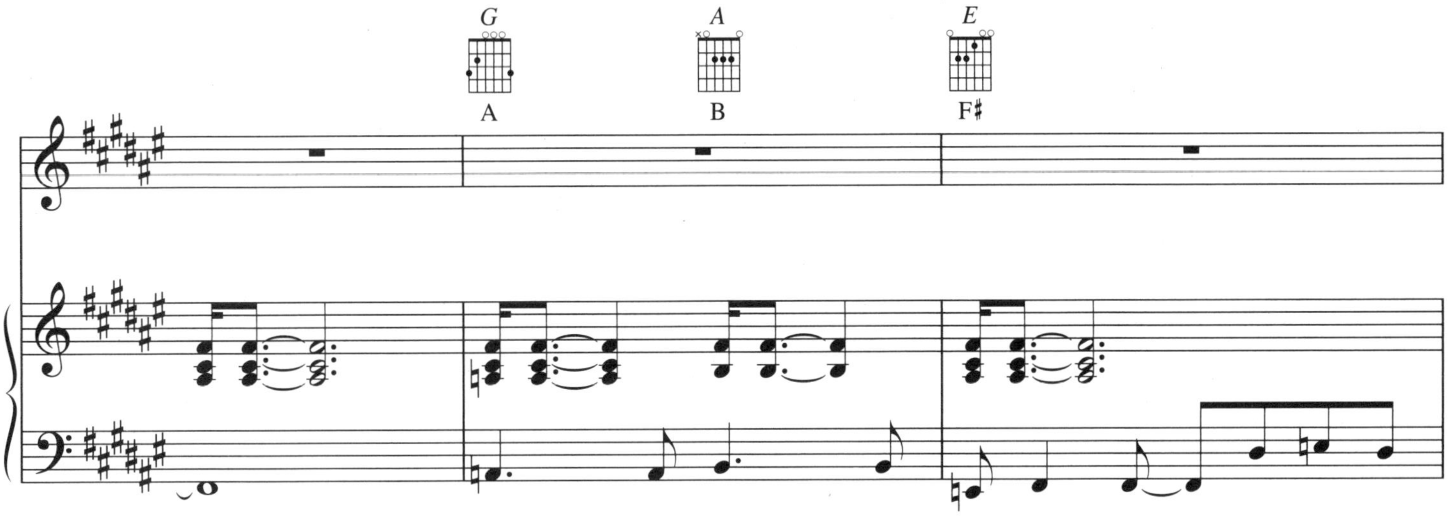

Chorus 3:
There's a club if you'd like to go.
You could meet somebody who really loves you.
So you go and you stand on your own.
And you leave on your own, and you go home.
And you cry, and you want to die.

Chorus 4:
When you say it's gonna happen "now,"
Well, when exactly do you mean?
See, I've already waited too long,
And all my hope is gone.

Chorus 5:
(Instrumental)

I BELONG TO YOU (+ MON COEUR S'OUVRE A TA VOIX)

Words and Music by
MATTHEW BELLAMY

♩ = 108

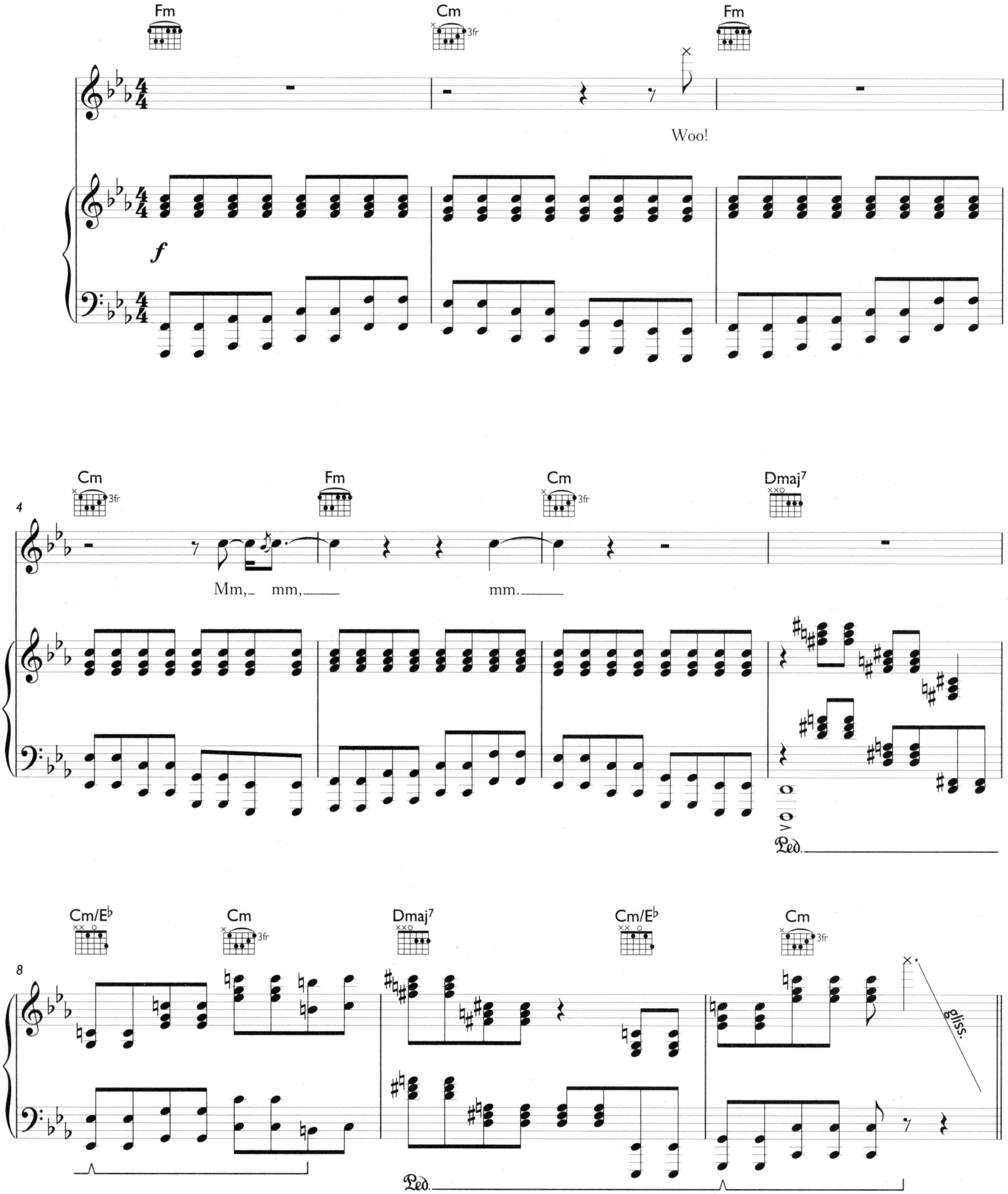

Fm
Cm
Fm
1. When these pil - lars get pulled down, it will be you
cont. sim.
Cm
Fm
Cm
who wears the crown and I'll owe ev - 'ry - thing to you.
Dmaj7
Cm/E♭
Cm
Dmaj7
Cm/E♭
Cm
Ooh, woah, ooh.
gliss.

Fm
Cm
3fr
Fm
21
How much pain has cracked your soul? How much love
2. Then she at - tacks me like a Le - o, when my heart
cont. sim.
Cm
3fr
Fm
Cm
3fr
24
could make you whole? You're my gui - ding light - ning strike.
is split like Ri - o, but, I as - sure you my debts are real.
D
Gm
3fr
E♭
3fr
B♭
27
I can't find the words to say, but they're o -
I can't find the words to say, when I'm
con Ped.
D
Gm
3fr
E♭
3fr
31
- ver - due. I've travel - led half the world to
confused. I've travel - led half the world to

B♭
Dmaj7
Cm/E♭
Cm
34
say, I be-long to you. Ooh,
say, you are my mu... -u...
Ped.
1.
2.
rit.
Dmaj7
Cm/E♭
Cm
Cm
37
ooh, ooh.
gliss.
Ped.
Freely
Dmaj7
D
D/F♯
40
(Ah! Re-ponds, re-
f
pp
p

Gm6
A
D
44
-ponds a ma ten-dres - - se, Ver - - - - se-
cont. sim.
D/F♯
G/B
Gm6
47
3
-moi, ver-se-moi l'iv-res - - se.
A
A♯dim7
F♯/A♯
Bm
50
Re-ponds a ma ten-dres - - se, re-ponds a ma ten-
fff
6

Em/C♯
A/C♯
D
53
- dres - - - se.
Ah!
3
6
Bm
Em7
A7
55
Ver - se - moi l'iv - - - res - - - se.
p
D
D/F♯
Gm6
58
Oh, oh,
ff

A7 D D/F#
61
oh. Ver - - - - - se-moi, ver-
Gmaj7/B B♭dim7 A
64
-se-moi, l'iv-res - - - se, re-ponds a ma ten-
A#dim7 F#/A# Bm Em/C# A/C#
67
-dres - se, re - ponds a ma ten - dres - - se,
fff

D
Daug
Bm
Em7
A7
70
Ah! Ver - se - moi l'iv - res - se.
p
pp
D
Bm
Em7
74
And I be - long, I be - long to you,
8vb
A7
Dmaj7
77
a - lone.
(8)
Ped.

Tempo I
Cm/E♭
Cm
Dmaj7
Cm/E♭
Cm
79
...u...
...use.
gliss.
Ped.
Fm
Cm
Fm
Cm
82
bass clarinet solo
f
Fm
Cm
Dmaj7
86
Gm
E♭
B♭
89

92
D
Gm
3fr
E♭
3fr
Oh,
and I
can't
find
the words
to
95
B♭
D
Gm
3fr
say,
and they're o
-
ver - due.
Travel
-
led
98
E♭
3fr
B♭
Dmaj7
Cm/E♭
Cm
3fr
3
half
the world
to
say,
I be-long
to
you.
Ooh,
102
Dmaj7
Cm/E♭
Cm
3fr
rit.
Dmaj7
Freely
ooh.
3
3

IRON MAN

Words and Music by
FRANK IOMMI, JOHN OSBOURNE,
WILLIAM WARD and TERENCE BUTLER

Hard rock ♩ = 76

G5 F♯5 G5 F♯5 G5 F♯5 D5 E5 B5 D5 E5
Can he see or is he blind? Can he walk at all,
G5 F♯5 G5 F♯5 G5 F♯5 D5 E5 B5 D5 E5
or if he moves, will he fall?
G5 F♯5 G5 F♯5 G5 F♯5 D5 E5 B5 D5 E5
Is he a-live or dead?
G5 F♯5 G5 F♯5 G5 F♯5 D5 E5 B5 D5 E5
Has he thoughts with - in his head? We'll just pass him there.

G5 F#5 G5 F#5 G5 F#5 D5 E5
10 9 10 9 10 9 5 7
N.C.
Why should we e - ven care?
B5 D5 E5
2 5 7
G5 F#5 G5 F#5 G5 F#5 D5 E5 B5 D5 E5
10 9 10 9 10 9 5 7 2 5 7
G5 F#5 G5 F#5 G5 F#5 D5 E5 B5 D5 E5
10 9 10 9 10 9 5 7 2 5 7
He was turned to steel
Now the time is here
Heav - y boots of lead

G5 F♯5 G5 F♯5 G5 F♯5 D5 E5 B5 D5 E5
in the great mag - net - ic field when he trav - elled time
for I - ron Man to spread fear, ven - geance from the grave,
fills his vic - tims full of dread. Run - ning as fast as they can,
G5 F♯5 G5 F♯5 G5 F♯5 D5 E5
To Coda
for the fu - ture of man - kind. No-bod-y wants him,
kills the peo - ple he once saved. No-bod-y wants him,
I - ron Man lives a - gain.
D5 B5
he just stares at the world,
they just turn their heads.
E5
plan-ning his ven - geance
No - bod - y helps him,

D5
B5
that__ he will__ soon un - furl.____
now__ he has__ his re - venge.____
1.
2.
Faster ♩ = 169
N.C.
simile
C♯5
Guitar solo ad lib....

N.C.
simile
B5
1.
2.
D.S. 𝄋 al Coda
(Tempo I)
Coda
N.C.
Faster 𝅗𝅥 = 156
1.2.3.
4.

IF TODAY WAS YOUR LAST DAY

Gtr. tuned down 1/2 step:
⑥ = E♭ ③ = G♭
⑤ = A♭ ② = B♭
④ = D♭ ① = E♭

Words and Music by
CHAD KROEGER

Moderately ♩ = 96

C#m
Cm
E
E♭
right. Leave no stone un - turned, leave your fears be - hind,
fight. Ev - 'ry sec - ond counts 'cause there's no sec - ond try,
Bsus
B♭sus
and try to take the path less trav - eled
so live it like you'll nev - er live it
C#m
Cm
E
E♭
by. That first step you take is the lon - gest stride.
twice. Don't take the free ride in your own life.
Bsus
B♭sus
If to - day was your last day

Chorus:

A
A♭
E
E♭
and to - mor - row was too late,
could you say good - bye to yes - ter - day?
B
B♭
(Would you? Would you?)
Would you live each mo-ment like your last,
A
A♭
E
E♭
leave old pic-tures in the past,
do - nate ev - 'ry dime you had...
B
B♭
1.
F♯7(4)
F7(4)
(Would you? Would you?)
if to - day was your last day?

C#m
Cm
E
E♭
Bsus
B♭sus
(If to - day was your last day.
2.
Bsus
B♭sus
A
A♭
And would you call on friends you nev - er see,
rem - i - nisce old mem - o - ries,
E
E♭
B
B♭
would you for - give your en - e - mies?
(Would you? Could you?)

A
A♭
And would you find that one you're dream - ing of, swear up and down to God a - bove
E
E♭
that you'd fi - nal - ly fall in love...
B
B♭
(Fi - nal - ly fall in love.
F♯7(4)
F7(4)
)
if to - day was your last day?
F♯5
F5
If to - day was your last day,
Bridge:
E
E♭
would you make your mark

Bsus
B♭sus
F♯
F
by mend - ing a bro - ken heart?
E
E♭
You know it's nev - er too late to shoot for the stars
Bsus
B♭sus
F♯
F
re - gard - less of who you are.
E
E♭
So do what - ev - er it takes 'cause you can't re - wind

Bsus
B♭sus
F♯
F
a mo - ment in this life.
E
E♭
Let noth - in' stand in your way 'cause the hands of time
Bsus
B♭sus
F♯
F
are nev - er on your side.
Chorus:
A2
A♭2
If to - day was your last day and to - mor - row was too late,

E
E♭
Bsus
B♭sus
could you say good - bye to yes - ter - day?
A
A♭
Would you live each moment like your last, leave old pic-tures in the past,
E
E♭
B
B♭
do - nate ev - 'ry dime you had.
(Would you? Would you?)
A
A♭
And would you call on friends you nev - er see, rem - i - nisce old mem - o - ries,

E
E♭
B
B♭
— would you for - give your en - e - mies? —
(Could you? Could you?)
A
A♭
And would you find that one you're dream - ing of, — swear up and down to God — a - bove —
E
E♭
B
B♭
— that you'd fi - nal - ly fall — in love... —
(Would you? Would you?)
F♯7(4)
F7(4)
if to - day was your — last day? —

KARMA POLICE

Words and Music by
THOMAS YORKE, JONATHAN GREENWOOD,
PHILIP SELWAY, COLIN GREENWOOD
and EDWARD O'BRIEN

Slowly ♩ = 76

Em G Am(9) D
he buzz - es like a fridge, he's like a de -
G D/F♯ C Bm Am Bm D
tuned ra - di - o.
Verses 2 & 3:
Am D9/F♯ Em G Am(9) F
2. Kar - ma po - lice, ar - rest this girl, her Hit - ler hair -
3. Kar - ma po - lice, I've giv-en all I can, it's not e - nough.
Em G Am(9) D
do is mak - ing me feel ill and we have crashed
I've giv - en all I can, but we're still on

G D/F♯ C Bm Am Bm D
her par - ty.
the pay - roll.
C D/A G F♯7 C D/A
This is what you get,
this is what you get,
mp
G F♯7 C D/A G Bm/F♯
this is what you get when you mess with us.
1. 2.
C Bm D C Bm/F♯ D
cresc.
cresc.

Chorus:
Bm D G D G D
For a min - ute there,
2. For a min - ute there,
I lost my - self, I lost my - self.
E9 Bm D G D
Phew, for a min - ute there, I lost my - self,
1.
G D E9 Bm D
I lost my - self.
mf
G D G D E9

2.
G
D
E9
I lost my - self.
Bm
D
G
D
G
D
E9
Bm
D
G
D
G
D
E9
Bm

KASHMIR

Gtr. tuned in DADGAD
⑥ = D ③ = G
⑤ = A ② = A
④ = D ① = D

Words and Music by
JIMMY PAGE, ROBERT PLANT
and JOHN BONHAM

Moderately ♩ = (80)

D6(♭3)
D7(♭3)
time and space, to be where I have been.
to that place, with yel - low des - ert screen.
D5
D5
B♭/D
D6(♭3)
To sit with el - ders of a gen - tle race this world has
My Shan - gri - la be - neath the sum - mer moon, I will re -
D7(♭3)
D5
D5
B♭/D
sel - dom seen, who talk of days for which they
turn a - gain, sure as the dust that blows high
D6(♭3)
D7(♭3)
sit in wait, when all will be re - vealed.
in June when mov - ing through Kash - mir.

G D F C D A C G B♭ F Dm
G D F C D A C G B♭ F Dm
B♭/D D6(♭3) D7(♭3)
D5 D5 B♭/D D6(♭3)
Talk and songs from tongues of lilt - ing grace, sounds ca -
Oh, fa - ther of the four winds, fill my sails, 'cross the

D7(♭3) D5 D5 B♭/D
ressed my ear.__ Though not a word__ I heard could I__
sea of years,__ with no pro - vi - sion but an o -
D6(♭3) D7(♭3)
__ re - late,__ the sto - ry was quite clear.__
pen face__ to flaunt__ the straits of fear.__
D5 D5 B♭/D D6(♭3)
Oh, whoa.__
Oh, whoa.__
D7(♭3) D5 D5 B♭/D
Oh, whoa.__
Oh, whoa.__

D6(♭3)
D7(♭3)
G D F C D A C G B♭ F Dm
G D F C D A C G B♭ F Dm
B♭/D
D6(♭3)
D7(♭3)
To Coda
(♪ = ♪)
G D F C D A C G B♭ Dm

A5
Ooh
Ba-by, I been fly - in'.
No, yeah.
Ma-ma cares, ain't no de - ny - ing.
Oh!

Ooh yes, I've been fly - ing.
My Ma - ma, ain't
no de - ny - ing, no de - ny - ing.
G D F C D A C G B♭ F Dm
12 11 10 9 7 6 5 4

G D F C D A C G B♭ F Dm
12 11 10 9 7 6 5 4
Oh!
G5
5
A5
7
All I see turns to brown,
as the sun burns the
ground.
And my eyes
3

A5
fill with sand
G5
A5
as I scan this wa - sted land,
G5
trying to find,
A5
trying to find where I've been.

D5
B♭/D
D6(♭13)
D7(♭13)
Oh.
D5
D5
B♭/D
D6(♭13)
D7(♭13)
D.S. 𝄋 al Coda
Coda
G D F C D A C G B♭ F Dm
G D F C D A C G B♭ F Dm
G5
A5
Oh! When I'm on, when I'm on my way, yeah!

G5
When I see,
when I see the way you
A5
stay.
Yeah!
G5
A5
G5
A5
G5
Ooh yeah,
ooh yeah. When I'm

A5
G5
down.
Ooh yeah,
A5
ooh yeah. When I'm down, so down.
G5
Ooh, my ba - by,
ooh, my ba-by, let me take you
A5
Repeat ad lib. and fade
there.

LAYLA

Words and Music by
ERIC CLAPTON and JIM GORDON

Moderate rock ♩ = 116

Verse:
C♯m
G♯m
1. (A) what - 'll you do___ when you get lone - ly,___
2. I tried to give you_______ con - so - la - tion_
3. So, make the best of___ the sit - u - a - tion,_
C♯m
C7
D7
E7
and no - bod - y's wait - in' by your_____ side?
when your__ old man,__ he let you_____ down.
be - fore__ I fi - n'lly go in - sane.
F♯m
B
E
A
You've been run - nin' and hid - ing much__ too long.____
Like a fool,_____ I fell in love__ with you.____
Please don't say_____ we'll nev - er find__ a way____
F♯m
B
E
N.C.
You know it's just__ your fool - ish pride.
You turned my whole__ world up - side down.
or tell me all___ my love's__ in vain.
Lay -

Chorus:
Dm
B♭
C
Dm
la, you got me on my knees. Lay -
B♭
C
Dm
la, I beg you, dar - ling, please. Lay -
B♭
C
Dm
la, dar - lin', won't you ease my wor-ried
B♭
C
1.2.
mind?

3.
Dm
B♭
C
Lay - la, you
got me on my knees. Lay - la, I
beg you, dar - ling, please. Lay - la,
dar - lin', won't you ease my wor-ried mind?

B♭
C
Dm
C
(Guitar)
Repeat as desired for solos
Last time
Dm
Interlude:
C
C/E
F
mp
C
C/E
F
mf

B♭9(♭5)
C
C/E
F
B♭9(♭5)
C
Am
Dm
G
C
Am
D
G

C
C/E
F
1.
2.
C
C/E
F
B♭9(♭5)
C
C
C/E
F
Repeat as desired for solos
B♭9(♭5)
C
rit. e dim.
mp

SYMPATHY FOR THE DEVIL

Words and Music by
MICK JAGGER and KEITH RICHARDS

A
E
man - y a man's soul and faith.
saw it was a time for a change.
D
I was a-round when Je - sus Christ had his
Killed the Tzar and his min-is - ters; An-a - sta -
A
E
mo - ment of doubt and pain.
sia screamed in vain.
D
Made damn sure that Pi - late washed his
I rode a tank, held a gen - 'ral's rank when the blitz-

A
E
Esus
E
hands
and sealed His
fate.
krieg
raged
and the bod - ies
stank.
Chorus:
B
B
A
Pleased to meet you,
hope you guess my
E
A/E
E
B
E/B
name.
Oh yeah.
Ah
But
what's puz-zling you is the
1.
B
A
E
Esus
E
na - ture of my game.

2.
B
A
E
A/E
E
Esus
na-ture of my game. Oh, yeah.
Verse 3:
E
D
3. I watched with glee while your kings and queens fought for ten-
A
E
Esus
E
decades for the gods they made. I
D
shout-ed out, "Who killed the Ken-ne-dys?" when

A
E
Esus
E
af - ter all it was you and me.
D
Let me please in - tro - duce my - self, I'm a man
A
E
Esus
E
of wealth and taste.
D
And I lay traps for trou - ba - dours who get

A
E
Esus
E
killed be-fore_ they reach_ Bom - bay._
Chorus:
B
A
E
Esus
Pleased to meet_ you, hope_ you guessed my name, oh
E
B
E/B
B
A
yeah._ But what's puz-zling you___ is the na - ture of___ my
E
Esus
E
Esus
E
game, oh___ yeah.__ Well, get down, hit it.

E7
D7
A7
Guitar solo
E7
D7
A7
E7
D7
A7
E7

D7
A7
E7
E
Chorus:
B
A
E
Esus
Pleased to meet you, hope you guess my name.
E
B
E/B
B
A
But what's con - fus - in' you is just the na-ture of my

E A/E E Esus
game. 4. Just as
Verse 4:
E D A7
ev-'ry cop is a crim-i-nal and all the sin-ners, saints,
E7 E D
as heads is tails, just call me Lu-ci-fer 'cause I'm in need
A E Esus E E7
of some re-straint. So if you meet me, have some cour-

D
A
E
te - sy,__ have some sym-pa-thy__ and some taste. Use
D
all your well__ learned pol - i - tesse_ or I'll
A
E
lay your soul to waste.__
Chorus:
B
A
E
Esus
Pleased to meet_ you,____ hope you guess_ my name.

E
B
A
But what's puz-zling you is the na-ture of my
E
A/E
E
Esus
E
game.
E7
D7
A7
E7
Repeat ad lib. and fade

LOSING MY RELIGION

Words and Music by
WILLIAM BERRY, PETER BUCK,
MICHAEL MILLS and MICHAEL STIPE

Em
lengths that I will go to, the dis-tance in your eyes.
try - ing to keep an eye on you like a hurt,
Am
Em
lost and blind - ed fool, fool.
Oh no, I've
Oh no, I've
Dm
said too much.
said too much.
I set it up.
I set it up.
G
Am
1.,3. That's me in the cor - ner.
2. Con-sid - er this, con -

Em
That's me in the spot - light los - ing my re - lig -
sid - er this __ the hint of the cen - tu - ry. ____ Con - sid - er this_
Am
Em
ion try - ing to keep __ up __ with you __
__ the slip ___ that brought me to my knees_
Am
__ and I don't __ know if I can do it.
___ failed. ____ What if all __ these fan - ta - sies __ come
Em
Dm
Oh no, I've said too __ much. _ I
flail - ing a - round? _ And now, I've said

G
have - n't said e - nough.
too much.
I thought that I heard you laugh -
F
G
Am
ing. I thought that I heard you sing.
F
Dm7
G
To Coda
I think I thought I saw you try.
Am
G
1
2
Ev - er - y whis -

Am
Am/G
Fmaj7
Am/G
C
Dm
But that was just a dream._
C
Dm
D.S. al Coda
That was just a dream._ That's me in the cor-
CODA
Am
F
Dm7
G
Am
But that was just a dream._ Try._

F
Cry. Why? Try. That was just a dream,
Dm7 G Am G
just a dream, just a dream, dream.
Am
1
2
rit.

MY GENERATION

Moderately fast ♩ = 184

Words and Music by
PETER TOWNSHEND

*Recording sounds one whole step lower than written. (Recording was slowed down.)
Tune down 1 whole step to play along with recording.

A
G
N.C.
A
G
A/G
G/A
Hope I die be - fore I get old.
This is my gen - er -
(Talk - in' 'bout my gen - er - a - tion.)
A
G
A/G
G/F
A
G
A/G
G/A
a - tion, this is my gen - er - a - tion, ba - by.
Verse 2:
A
G
N.C.
A
G
A/G
G/A
2. Why don't you all f - fade a - way?
(Talk - in' 'bout my gen - er - a - tion.)
A
G
N.C.
A
G
A/G
G/A
Don't try and dig what we all say.
I'm
(Talk - in' 'bout my gen - er - a - tion.)

A G
N.C.
A G
A/G G/A
not tryin' to cause a big s-sen-sa-tion,
I'm just
(Talk-in' 'bout my gen-er-a-tion.)
talk-in' 'bout my g-gen-er-a-tion.
This is my gen-er-
(Talk-in' 'bout my gen-er-a-tion.)
a-tion,
this is my gen-er-a-tion, ba-by.
(Bass solo)
3

A N.C. A A/G
G G G/A
A N.C. A A/G
G G G/A
A N.C. A A/G
G G G/A
A A/G A A/G
G G/A G G/A
My, my, my, my, my gen - er, my, my, my.
Verse 3:
B N.C. B B/A
A A A/G
3. Why don't you all f - fade a - way? Yeah,
(Talk - in' 'bout my gen - er - a - tion.)

B A N.C. B A B/A A/G
don't try to dig what we all s - s - s - s - s - s say. I'm
(Talk - in' 'bout my gen - er - a - tion.)
B A N.C. B A B/A A/G
not try-in' to cause no big sen - sa - tion, I'm just
(Talk-in' 'bout my gen - er - a - tion.)
B A N.C. B A B/A A/G
talk - in' 'bout my gen - er - a - tion. This is my gen - er -
(Talk - in' 'bout my gen - er - a - tion.)
B A B7sus/A A7sus/G B A B7sus/A A7sus/G
a - tion, this is my gen - er - a - tion, ba - by.

B B7sus/A B B7sus/A
A A7sus/G A A7sus/G
My, my gen, gen - er - a - tion, my, my, my.
C C/B♭ C C/B♭
B♭ B♭/A♭ B♭ B♭/A♭
My gen - er - a - tion.
Verse 4:
C N.C. C C/B♭
B♭ B♭ B♭/A♭
4. Peo - ple try to put us down,
(Talk - in' 'bout my gen - er - a - tion.)
C N.C. C C/B♭
B♭ B♭ B♭/A♭
just be-cause we get a - round.
(Talk - in' 'bout my gen - er - a - tion.)

C
Bb
N.C.
C
Bb
C/Bb
Bb/Ab
Things they do look awful c - cold,
yeah.
(Talk - in' 'bout my gen - er - a - tion.)
C
Bb
N.C.
C
Bb
C/Bb
Bb/Ab
Hope I die be - fore I get old.
It's my gen - er -
(Talk - in' 'bout my gen - er - a - tion.)
C
Bb
C7sus/Bb
Bb7sus/Ab
C
Bb
C7sus/Bb
Bb7sus/Ab
a - tion, this is my gen - er - a - tion, ba - by.
C
Bb
C7sus/Bb
Bb7sus/Ab
C
Bb
C7sus/Bb
Bb7sus/Ab
My, my, my gen - er - a - tion.

D D7sus/C D D7sus/C D D7sus/C
C C7sus/B♭ C C7sus/B♭ C C7sus/B♭
Talk-in' 'bout,
it's my gen-er - a - tion, my gen-er - a - tion, it's my gen-er -
a - tion, ba - by. It's my gen-er - a - tion, this is my gen-er -
a - tion, this is my gen-er - a - tion, this is my gen-er - a - tion.

PAINT IT, BLACK

Words and Music by
MICK JAGGER and KEITH RICHARDS

Dm
Fm
black._ No col-ors an-y-more_ I
black,_ with flow-ers and my love_ both
black._ I see my red door, I___ must
A
C
want them to turn black._
nev-er to come back._
have it paint-ed black._
Bridges 1, 2, 3, & 5:
Dm C
Fm E♭
1.5. I see the
2. I see peo-ple
3. May-be then I'll
loco
F C Dm
A♭ E♭ Fm
girls walk by___ dressed in_____ their sum-mer clothes,_
turn their heads_ and quick-ly look_ a-way,___
fade a-way__ and not___ have to face__ the facts.___
To Coda
1.2.
C F C G A
E♭ A♭ E♭ B♭ C
I have to turn my head_ un-til_____ my dark-ness goes.____
like a new-born ba-by, it___ just hap-pens ev-'ry day.____
It's not eas-y fac-ing up___ when your___ whole world is black._

3.
Verse 4:
A
C
Dm
Fm
4. No more will my green sea go
turn a deep - er blue.
I could not
fore - see this thing hap - pen - ing to you.
Bridge 4:
Dm C F C Dm
Fm E♭ A♭ E♭ Fm
4. If I look hard e - nough in - to the set - ting sun,

C F C G A
E♭ A♭ E♭ B♭ C
D.S. 𝄋 al Coda
my love will laugh with me before the mornin' comes.
𝄌 Coda
A Dm
C Fm
Mm.
8vb throughout
A Dm
C Fm
build
Mm.
(8vb)
A
C

Dm
Fm
A
C
Mm.
Dm
Fm
Mm.
A
C
Dm
Fm
I wan-na see your face
A
C
paint - ed black, black as night, black as coal. Don't

Dm
Fm
A
C
wan-na see the sun
fly-ing high in the sky.
Dm
Fm
I wan-na see it paint-ed, paint-ed, paint-ed, paint-ed
A
C
black, yeah.
Dm
Fm
Mm.
A
C
Repeat and fade

RIGHT NOW

Words and Music by
SAMMY HAGAR, ALEX VAN HALEN,
MICHAEL ANTHONY and EDWARD VAN HALEN

B♭
C2
Dm
Dsus
Dm
D2
C
Csus
C
B♭
Dm
C
F
G
B♭
C
Dm
Dsus
Dm
D2
C
Csus
C
B♭
Dm
C
F
G
B♭
C
Dm
Dsus
Dm
D2
C
Csus
C
B♭
Dm

1.
C F G B♭ C
2.
C B♭ Am Gm F Dm
Verse:
C B♭
1. Don't wan - na wait_ till to - mor - row.
2. See additional lyrics
A5 G5 A5 G5 A5 C6 Dm
Why put it off an - oth - er day?___
C B♭
One by one, girl, prob - lems build up__

A5 G5 A5 G5 A5 C6 B♭
and stand in our way.
Oh!
Pre-chorus:
C F G B♭
1. One step a - head, one step be - hind it.
2. See additional lyrics
(3.) now. (Inst. solo ad lib....
C Dm
Now, you got - ta run to get e - ven.
B♭ C F G B♭
Make fu - ture plans, don't live a - bout yes - ter - day, hey!

C
Asus
A
Come on, turn, turn this thing a - round. Right
Chorus:
F
F/A
B♭
C7sus
C
now! Hey, it's your to - mor - row. Right
F
F/A
B♭
C7sus
C
now! Come on, it's ev - 'ry - thing. Right
F
F/A
B♭
C7sus
C
To Coda
now! Catch your mag - ic mo-ment, do it right here and now.

B♭2
1.
2.
It means ev - 'ry - thing.
It means ev - 'ry - thing.
Dm
It's en - light - en - ing.
B♭
Right now.
Dm
Ah, what are you wait - in' for?

B♭
C2
Oh, ___
F5
G5
B♭
C2
yeah. ___
A
D.S. 𝄋 al Coda
Right
𝄌 Coda
F
F/A
B♭
C7sus
C
___ Oh, ___ right now. ___

Verse 2:
Miss a beat, you lose the rhythm,
And nothing falls into place.
Only missed by a fraction,
Sent a little off your pace.

Pre-chorus 2:
The more things you get, the more you want,
Just tradin' one for the other.
Workin' so hard to make it easy.
Got to turn, come on, turn this thing around.
(To Chorus:)

SMELLS LIKE TEEN SPIRIT

Words and Music by
DAVE GROHL, KURT COBAIN
and KRIST NOVOSELIC

Moderate rock ♩ = 112

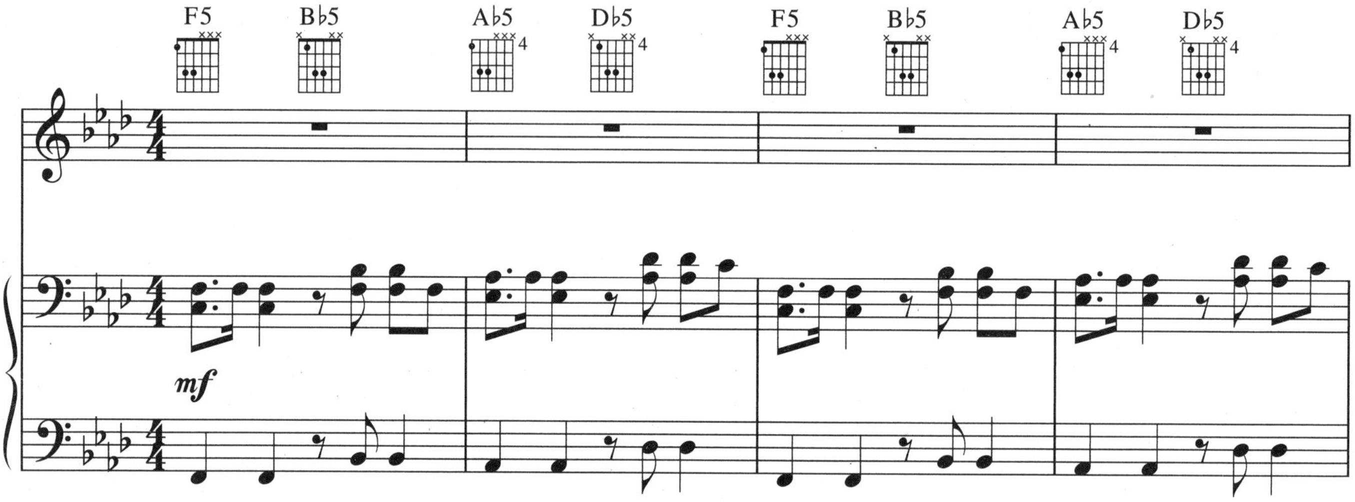

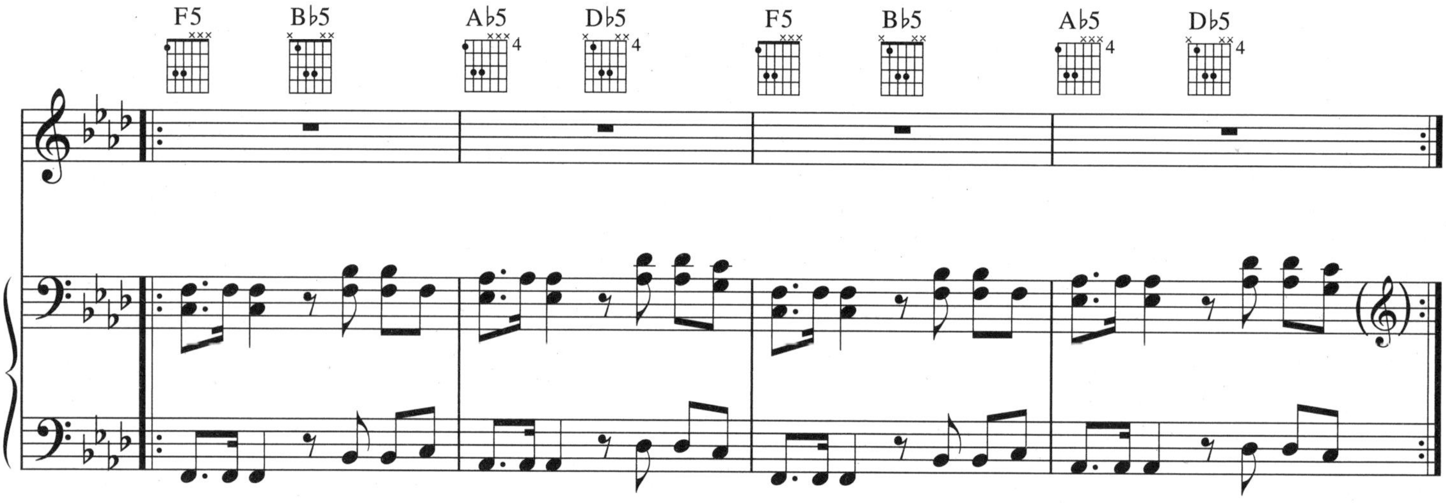

Verse:
1. Load up on guns, bring your friends. It's fun to lose
2. I'm worse at what I do best, and for this gift
3. And I for - get just why I taste. Oh yeah, I guess
and to pre - tend. She's o - ver bored, and self - as - sured.
I feel blessed. Our lit - tle group has al - ways been
it makes me smile. I found it hard, it was hard to find.
Oh no, I know a dirt - y word.
and al - ways will un - til the end.
Oh well, what - ev - er, nev - er mind.
Hel - lo, hel - lo,
F5
B♭5
mf
A♭5
D♭5
F5
B♭5
A♭5
D♭5
hel - lo. How low? Hel - lo, hel - lo, hel - lo. How low?

F5 B♭5 A♭5 D♭5 F5 B♭5
Hel - lo, hel - lo, hel - lo. How low? Hel - lo, hel - lo,
Chorus:
A♭5 D♭5 F5 B♭5 A♭5 D♭5
hel - lo. With the lights out it's less dan - g'rous. Here we are
f
F5 B♭5 A♭5 D♭5 F5 B♭5
now, en - ter - tain us. I feel stu - pid and con - ta -
A♭5 D♭5 F5 B♭5 A♭5 D♭5
gious. Here we are now, en - ter - tain us. A mu - lat -

To Coda
F5
B♭5
A♭5
D♭5
E5
G♭5
to, an al - bi - no, a mos - qui - to, my li - bi -
do. Yeah! Yay.
Yay.
1.
N.C.
mp

2.
F5 B♭5 A♭5 D♭5 F5 B♭5 A♭5 D♭5
(Inst. solo….
F5 B♭5 A♭5 D♭5 F5 B♭5 A♭5 D♭5
F5 B♭5 A♭5 D♭5 F5 B♭5 A♭5 D♭5
F5 B♭5 A♭5 D♭5 F5 B♭5 A♭5 D♭5

D.S. 𝄋 al Coda
N.C.
mp
…end solo)
Coda
Ab5 Db5 F5 Bb5 Ab5 Db5
do. A de - ni - al, a de - ni - al. A de - ni -
F5 Bb5 Ab5 Db5 F5 Bb5
al, a de - ni - al. A de - ni - al, a de - ni -
Ab5 Db5 F5 Bb5 Ab5 Db5 F5
al. A de - ni - al, a de - ni - al. A de - ni - al.

THE SPIRIT OF RADIO

Words by
NEIL PEART

Music by
GEDDY LEE and ALEX LIFESON

A
B(add E)
E
B(add E)
E/G♯
A
N.C.
E
B(add E)
Be - gin the day with a friend - ly voice, a com-
E/G♯
A
B
E
pan - ion un - ob - tru - sive. Plays that song that's
B(add E)
E/G♯
A
B
so e - lu - sive, and the mag - ic mu - sic makes your morn - ing mood.

E
B(add E)
E/G♯
A
N.C.
E
B
Emaj7/G♯
Off on your way. Hit the o - pen road. There is mag - ic at your fin -
A
B
E
B
gers. For the Spir - it ev - er lin - gers, un - de -
Emaj7/G♯
A
B
E
mand - ing con - tact in your hap - py sol - i - tude.

B(add E)
E/G#
A
B(add E)
In -
N.C.
vis - i - ble air - waves crack - le with life.
Bright an - ten - nae bris - tle with the en - er - gy.
E -

mo - tion - al feed - back on a time - less wave - length,
bear - ing a gift — be - yond price, al - most —
free.
E
B
All this ma - chin - er - y, mak - ing mod - ern mu - sic, can

E/G♯ A B E
still be o-pen-heart-ed. Not so cold-ly chart-ed, it's real-
B E/G♯ A B
ly just a ques-tion of your hon-es-ty.
E B E/G♯
One likes to be-lieve in the free-dom of mu-sic,
A B E B
but glit-ter-ing priz-es and end-less com-pro-mis-es

E/G♯
A
B
E
shat-ter the il - lu-sion of in - teg-ri - ty.
D/F♯
E/G♯
D/F♯
A little faster
E
A
B
"For the
E
A
B
E
words of the prof-its were writ-ten on the stu-di-o wall,

A
B
N.C.
con - cert hall;
E
A
B
E
A
B
N.C.
ech-oes with the sounds of sales - men."
E

STAIRWAY TO HEAVEN

Words and Music by
JIMMY PAGE and ROBERT PLANT

C D Fmaj7 Am C D Fmaj7
1. There's a
Verse 1:
Am E+/G♯ C/G D/F♯ Fmaj7
la - dy who's sure all that glit - ters is gold, and she's buy - ing a stair - way to
G/B Am Am E+/G♯ C/G D/F♯
heav - en. When she gets there, she knows if the stores are all closed, with a
Fmaj7 G/B Am C D
word she can get what she came for. Ooo,

Fmaj7 Am C G Dsus D
ooo,___ ooo,_ and she's buy - ing a stair - way_ to heav - en. There's a
C D Fmaj7 Am C D
sign on the wall,_ but she wants to be sure,_ 'cause you know some - times words have two
Fmaj7 Am E+/G♯ C/G D/F♯
mean - ings. In a tree by the brook,_ there's a song - bird_ who sings,_ some - times
Fmaj7 G/B Am Am E+/G♯
all of_ our thoughts are mis - giv - en.

C/G
D/F♯
Fmaj7
G/B
Am
G/B
Slightly faster
Am7
Dsus
D
Am7
Em/D
Ooo, it makes me won - der.
D
C/D
D
Am7
Dsus
D
Ooo, makes me won - der.
Am7
Em/D
D
C/D
D
2. There's a

Verses 2 & 3:
C G/B Am C G/B Fmaj7
feel - ing I get when I look to the west, and my spir - it is cry - ing for leav -
whis - pered that soon if we all call the tune, then the pip - er will lead us to rea -
Am C G/B Am
ing. In my thoughts I have seen rings of smoke through the trees, and the
son. And a new day will dawn, for those who stand long, and the
C G/B Fmaj7 Am C G/B
voic - es of those who stand look - ing.
for - ests will ech - o with laugh - ter.
Am7 Dsus D Am7 Em/D
Ooh, it makes me won - der.

D C/D D Am7 Dsus D
Ooo, it real-ly makes me won - der.
Am7 Em/D 1. D C/D D 2. D C/D D
3. And it's
accel.
Faster (♩ = 88)
Verses 4 & 5:
C G/B Am C G/B Fmaj7
4. If there's a bus - tle in your hedge-row, don't be a-larmed now, it's just a spring clean for the May
5. Your head is hum-ming and it won't go, in case you don't know, the pip-er's call - ing you to join
mf
Am C G/B Am
Queen. Yes, there are two paths you can go by, but in the long run,
him. Dear la - dy, can you hear the wind blow, and did you know,

C
G/B
Fmaj7
Am
C
G/B
there's still time to change_the road___ you're on.___
your stair - way lies on the___ whis - p'rin' wind.__
1.
Am7
Dsus
D
Am7
Em/D
And it makes me won - der,
D
C/D
D
Am7
Dsus
D
ahh.
Am7
Em/D
D
C/D
D
2. D

D2 D Dsus D2 D Dsus D C(9) C(9)♯11 C(9) C(9)♯11 C(9)
f
D2 D Dsus D2 D Dsus D C(9) C(9)♯11 C(9) G/B
Guitar Solo:
Am C/G F Fmaj7 Am C/G
F Fmaj7 Am C/G F Fmaj7

Am
C/G
F
Fmaj7
Am
C/G
F
Fmaj7
6
Am
C/G
F
Fmaj7
6
Am
C/G
Fmaj7
Am
C/G
3

Fmaj7
Am
C/G
Fmaj7
Am
C/G
Fmaj7
Am
G
F
G
Am
G
And as we wind_ on down the road,__
our shad - ows tall - er than our soul.__
F
G
Am
G
F
G
There walks a la - dy we all know,______

Am G F G Am G
who shines white light and wants to show_ how ev - 'ry - thing_ still turns to
F G Am G F G
gold._____ And if you lis - ten ver - y hard,_____
Am G F G Am G Fmaj7
the tune will come to you_ at last._____ When all are one_ and one is all,_

Am
G
Fmaj7
to be a rock_ and not to roll._
Am
C/G
Fmaj7
Am
C/G
Fmaj7
Am
C/G
Fmaj7
Am
C/G
rit.
Fmaj7
N.C.
And she's buy - ing a stair - way_ to heav - en._
mf

UPRISING

♩. = 132

Tune guitar to:
6 = D (lowest string)

Words and Music by
MATTHEW BELLAMY

D5
5fr
18
(Repeat section x 4)
G5
5fr
1. Pa - ra - noi - a is in bloom, the P. R. trans - mis - sions
2. In - ter - chang - ing mind con - trol, come let the re - vo - lu - tion
(Play small notes 2° only
1° cont. sim. from previous vamp)
F5
A
6fr
22
will re - sume, they'll try to push drugs that keep us all dumbed down and hope that
take its toll, if you could flick the switch and o - pen your third eye, you'd see that
G5
5fr
Doct/F
3fr
Doct/C♯
D5
5fr
25
we will nev - er see the truth a - round. An - o - ther prom - ise, an - o - ther seed, an - o - ther
we should nev - er be a - fraid to die. Rise up and take the pow - er back, it's time the
(So come on.)

G5
F5
G#
A
29
pack-aged lie to keep us trapped in greed, and all the green belts wrapped a-
fat cats had a heart at-tack, they know that their time's com-ing
G5
Doct/F
Doct/C#
32
-round our minds and end-less red tape to keep the truth con-fined.
to an end, we have to uni-fy and watch our flag as-cend.
(So come on.)
Dm
35
mp
ff

39
(Sing B.Vox. 2° only)
Gm7
3fr
They will not force
(Play ossia 2 & 3°)
ff
F
A
42
us, they will stop de -
Gm
3fr
F6
A/C♯
Dm
45
- gra - - - ding us.
They will

Gm
F
G♯dim7
48
not con - - trol us,
A
Gm
F6
A/C♯
51
we will be vic - tor - - i - ous.
(So come on.)
1.
Doct
55
mp
f

2,3.
Doct
5fr
59
To Coda
pp
ff
63
G5
5fr
(Hey!
Hey!
Hey!
Doct/F
3fr
A
66
Hey!)
Gm
3fr
69
F
A/C♯

Doct
5fr
G5
5fr
(Hey!
Hey!
Hey!
Doct/F
3fr
A
Hey!)
(Play small notes instead 2°)
Gm
3fr
F
A/C#
(Play small notes 1° only)
Doct
7fr
D.% al Coda

Coda
Dm
Gm
3fr
F
G♯oct
6fr
81
p
ff
A
Gm
3fr
F
C♯oct
4fr
85
Doct
5fr
89
N.C.
(Hey!
Hey!
Hey!
Hey!)
p
ff
(L.H. sempre ff)

WHAT S THE FREQUENCY, KENNETH?

Words and Music by
WILLIAM BERRY, PETER BUCK,
MICHAEL MILLS and MICHAEL STIPE

1.
G A D A
Tun - nel vis - ion from the out - sid - er's screen. I nev - er un - der - stood
you said that iron - y was the shack - les of youth.
D G A G A
the fre - quen - cy, uh huh.
D A D G A
You wore our ex - pect - a - tions like an ar - mored suit, uh huh.
2.
G A D D A D G
You wore a shirt of vi - o - lent green, uh huh.

A G A D A
I nev - er un - der - stood
D G A G A D
the fre - quen - cy, uh huh.
Bm A Bm A
Guitar Solo ad lib.
Bm A G A D

A D Bm G A D
"What's the fre - quen - cy, Ken - neth?" is your Ben - ze drine, uh - huh.
A G A D Bm G
But - ter - fly de - cal, rear - view mir - ror, dog - ging the scene.
A D Bm E G
You smile like the car - toon,
A G A
tooth for a tooth. You said that iron - y was the shack - les of youth.

D A D G A
You wore a shirt of vi - o - lent green, uh huh.
G A D A D G
I nev - er un - der - stood the fre - quen - cy, uh huh.
A G A D A
You wore our ex - pect - a - tions
D G A G A
like an ar - mored suit, uh huh.
I could - n't un - der - stand.

D A D G A
You said that i - ro - ny was the shack - les of youth, uh huh.
G A D A D G
I could - n't un - der - stand. You wore a shirt of vi - o - lent green, uh huh.
A G A D A
I could - n't un - der - stand. I nev - er un - der - stood,
D G A G A D
don't fuck with me, uh huh.

TOM SAWYER

Words by
PYE DUBOIS and NEIL PEART

Music by
GEDDY LEE and ALEX LIFESON

Moderate rock 𝅗𝅥 **= 84**

E
D
Though his mind is not___ for rent, don't put him
No, his mind is not___ for rent to an - y
f
A7sus
down as ar - ro - gant. His re - serve, a qui - et de - fense,__
god or gov - ern - ment. Al - ways hope - ful, yet dis - con - tent,
C
N.C.
rid - ing out the day's__ e - vents: the riv - er.
he knows chang - es aren't per - ma - nent. But change is.
E
D
A7sus

N.C.
What you say__ a-bout his com-pa-ny__ is
And what you say__ a-bout his com-pa-ny__ is
what you say__ a-bout so-ci-e-ty.__ Catch the mist,__
what you say__ a-bout so-ci-e-ty.__ Catch the wit-ness,
catch the myth,_ catch the mys-t'ry, catch the drift.__
catch the wit,__ catch the spir-it, catch the spit.__

A5
B2
B5
A5
The world is, the world__ is. Love and
The world is, the world__ is. Love and
G2
B5
A5
G2
A5
life are deep, may - be as his skies are
life are deep, may - be as his eyes are
E5
To Coda
wide. To -
wide.

day's Tom Saw-yer, he gets high on you, and the space he in - vades, he gets by on you.
N.C.
(♩ = ♩)
Guitar solo ad lib.
N.C.

ff
E
D
A7sus
C
3
D.S. 𝄋 al Coda

Coda
Ex - it the war - ri - or. To - day's Tom Saw - yer, he gets
high on you and the en - er - gy you trade, he gets
F♯5
right on to the fric - tion of the day.
E5
F♯5
Repeat and fade